A Simple Path to a Miraculous Life

DEBRA CUMMINGS

BALBOA
PRESS
A DIVISION OF HAY HOUSE

Copyright © 2018 Debra Cummings.

All rights reserved. No part of this book may be used or reproduced by any means, graphic, electronic, or mechanical, including photocopying, recording, taping or by any information storage retrieval system without the written permission of the author except in the case of brief quotations embodied in critical articles and reviews.

Balboa Press books may be ordered through booksellers or by contacting:

Balboa Press
A Division of Hay House
1663 Liberty Drive
Bloomington, IN 47403
www.balboapress.com
1 (877) 407-4847

Because of the dynamic nature of the Internet, any web addresses or links contained in this book may have changed since publication and may no longer be valid. The views expressed in this work are solely those of the author and do not necessarily reflect the views of the publisher, and the publisher hereby disclaims any responsibility for them.

The author of this book does not dispense medical advice or prescribe the use of any technique as a form of treatment for physical, emotional, or medical problems without the advice of a physician, either directly or indirectly. The intent of the author is only to offer information of a general nature to help you in your quest for emotional and spiritual well-being. In the event you use any of the information in this book for yourself, which is your constitutional right, the author and the publisher assume no responsibility for your actions.

Any people depicted in stock imagery provided by Getty Images are models, and such images are being used for illustrative purposes only.
Certain stock imagery © Getty Images.

Print information available on the last page.

ISBN: 978-1-9822-0042-8 (sc)
ISBN: 978-1-9822-0044-2 (hc)
ISBN: 978-1-9822-0043-5 (e)

Library of Congress Control Number: 2018903112

Balboa Press rev. date: 04/10/2018

This book is dedicated to my wonderful and patient husband, Steve, and to my family who has always supported me. To Laura, Janine, and Kathy, who continued to believe in me whenever I lost sight.

Table of Contents

ix	Introduction: Create Improvement in Your Life—Beyond Reason
1	Chapter 1: You Are on Purpose
9	Chapter 2: What Is Your Story?
17	Chapter 3: Whether You Think You Can or Can't
25	Chapter 4: Who Do You Think You Are?
35	Chapter 5: Surrender to the Universe
43	Chapter 6: Explosive Jumps—Taking Quantum Leaps
53	Chapter 7: Attitude of Gratitude
59	Chapter 8: The Courage to Live Your Dreams
65	Chapter 9: Shaking Things Up
73	Chapter 10: Genuine Acceptance
79	Chapter 11: Magnificent Obsession—Fall in Love with Your Dreams
85	Conclusion: Feel Your Dream
89	About the Author
90	Bibliography

Introduction
Create Improvement in Your Life Beyond Reason

Introduction

Create Improvement in Your Life—Beyond Reason

We come from many different walks of life. Your upbringing in San Antonio, Texas, may be different from your friend's childhood in Portland, Maine. Your coworker may originally be from South Africa and return there quite often to connect with family. Your own children, not impressed by your stories of trekking through five feet of snow to get to school, are growing up with different experiences than you did. Our journeys, beliefs, and attitudes may be vastly different, and there are countless factors that determine how a person views the world. But one thing we all have in common is the desire to improve our lives.

No matter what your station in life, you have the need to makes things better, to be successful (and that definition depends on your own interpretation), to be happy, and to be at peace with your life. If you don't have a clue as to where to start, there are many websites and blogs dedicated to helping you find your way. They will tell you to "Face your fears!" or "Refine your goals!" or "Invest your profits!" or "Declutter your kitchen!" And while all of those may offer wise advice, especially if you're tripping over things in your kitchen, I'd like to offer you a simpler way.

A Simple Path to a Miraculous Life is focused on propelling you forward into a life of your dreams. That's right: propelling. If you let it, the Universe will change your life in monumental ways you can't even imagine. Forget the small, incremental steps. We're talking about huge change. This isn't about meekly writing down your goals and sitting idly by, hoping for a miracle. It's about taking action, being prepared to face uncomfortable situations, and having the courage to live your dreams (and that's just chapter 8). The Universe is here for you, and all you have to do is surrender to it. When you are genuinely open to its magnitude, you will experience an unbelievable quantum leap that will transform your life.

The Energy of Business

Even though I'm known as an energy practitioner and much of my work focuses on the inner self and awakening, people often come to me for business advice. You might find that surprising, but after all, creating a business is just like creating any other goal or dream you may have. I come from a very successful business family, and I struggled in the shadow of that for many years. I've been an entrepreneur all of my adult life, and I've experienced more failures than anyone I have ever known. The lessons I learned from all that failure taught me what doesn't work in life and what does. They led me to enormous personal success.

When I was much younger, about thirty-five or forty years ago, I had a tremendous inner drive to succeed. I didn't have much in the way of traditional education, and I rarely attended high school classes, finally dropping out at fifteen years old.

> *The lessons I learned from all that failure taught me what doesn't work in life and what does. They led me to enormous personal success.*

I had a unique business where I sold sewing machines through ads in the newspaper and at swap meets. Later, I hired other people to sell the machines for me in other locations. There was a lot of profit in the business, but it was not in alignment with who I was.

Somehow, I found my way into the wholesale clothing mart, which was really a difficult task. I started buying designer children's clothes and selling them out of my home, and then I began hosting home parties. I would carry racks of beautiful children's clothes to other people's homes. As part of the fun, I brought giveaways of small children's toys, pen sets, stationery, etc. The trinkets became so popular, I expanded that idea and let go of the clothing. I then hired others to also sell these children's trinkets at home parties.

I had plenty of inventory, and eventually I opened my first of a chain of stores. It was a small space and featured all small, fun items for children. The success of the products allowed me to expand to other locations. In one of the stores, I started a separate business teaching craft classes. I carried fabrics, paint, rubber stamps, beads, etc. Expanding the craft business, I was able to hire other people to teach, and then I developed my own line of children's craft projects.

My store was a really popular place for children's birthday parties. I later expanded the party business by hiring others to teach arts and crafts as entertainment at children's parties. Several schools also hired me to offer special craft classes to their students. During this time, and long before the internet, I began a mail-order business. I ran ads and shipped thousands of inexpensive trinkets and gifts for kids.

Several of my businesses brought in some revenue, but the majority failed. I was working long hours, seven days a week, so it wasn't for lack of trying. But no matter how hard I worked and how much I suffered, I was failing at an accelerating rate. I wasn't enjoying anything like the kind of success I had hoped for.

You see, everything I was trying to do came from a place of desperation. I just wanted a business of my own so I could earn a living and not have to send my young daughter to day care. At that point, I would do anything to achieve this goal, but the harder I fought, the less likely it seemed that I would be successful.

Finding the Secret to Success

I didn't know there was a *secret* to success. It took decades for me to discover it, and it is the road map I now follow. This book is all about that. It's about creating what you want as you navigate through life. I'll explain the law of attraction in chapter 2, "What Is Your Story?"

I'll help you change your thinking in chapter 3, "Whether You Think You Can or Can't." And I'll help you learn to trust Source, God, or the Universe in chapter 5, "Surrender to the Universe."

However you name the Power of Life is perfectly fine. We live with an invisible Creator that goes by many names. Some people call it God, Universe, or Source. This power is perfectly magnificent, and even trying to describe its existence with language seems to diminish the concept. But it is and always has been serving you. You communicate with it and direct it through your heart, your intentions, your emotions, your thoughts, and your words. You have been unconsciously communicating with this Creator all along. Are you happy with the outcome?

I am referring to the presence that you give credit to for the creation of the world, yourself included. I believe all religions and faiths have many elemental beliefs in common, so I think we can talk about how to improve our spiritual lives no matter what background we come from. Please translate any term I use into something that is more of a match for your own beliefs.

Whatever your beliefs, this book offers the opportunity to strengthen your connection with your faith in chapter 10, "Genuine Acceptance."

The miracles of life are available to each one of us, just waiting for us to call on them.

With *The Simple Path to a Miraculous Life*, I hope to inspire you to allow and receive all that life has to offer. Together, we will walk through the simple steps that attract life's magic to you. The miracles of life are available to each one of us, just waiting for us to call on them. I'd like to share with you some of the wisdom that supports me in my own life.

You Don't Have to Be Miserable

Many of you do enjoy your lives and are grateful for your friends and family. There are many aspects of your life that make you happy. Yet you know there's more out there for you or there's just something missing. And there are many of you who are really having a difficult time in life. You may feel miserable, depressed, despondent, hopeless, or at an end. If so, I can relate. I too have felt this way.

Earlier in my life, I had no sense of self. I felt completely powerless. Nothing in my life worked. Everything was a struggle, as if I was swimming against the tide. I had no control over my life. Things seemed to be done *to* me, not *by* me. Things never seemed to go my way. There was no way out.

I was afraid of absolutely everything. I lived with constant panic attacks. I'd have a panic attack if the phone rang. I didn't know how to support myself. I had no patience or ability as a parent, and I would get so angry at the smallest things. My life was completely out of control.

Did I show my broken life in public? Of course not. I had to be perfect—my hair, my makeup, my clothing, my state of mind. At least on the surface, everything had to be flawless. It was my way of staying safe in the world. If I were perfect, I would be liked and respected. I would have value. As you can imagine, such pretense took all of my energy. When I could no longer hide the depression and the anxiety and the feelings of worthlessness, the facade came crumbling down. Then I had a nervous breakdown.

The Power of Energy Work and Proper Use of the Mind

So how did I go from a despairing broken life to a life flowing with happiness and possibilities—a life filled with miracles? I discovered ways to change the story of my life through the use of energy work and proper use of the mind. You know what I mean by the story: it's that narrative inside your head that is constantly talking, nagging, judging, and criticizing as you go on about your day. For me, those thoughts were incredibly painful and self-defeating. But by using techniques such as "yes" meditation, I was able to change my life as well as the story of my life. I was moved to a higher level of consciousness where I viewed my life differently.

Energy techniques, or using your mind in the powerful way that was intended, can help you release the obstacles and the resistance you've built up since you were a child. By removing these barriers and raising your vibration, you can transform your life. There are many methods that can help you move to your next level of awareness—spiritually, consciously, and psychologically. What's important is that you follow what resonates with you.

This book offers information and several methods to help you gain a new perspective. I will teach you the steps that led me out of the deep, dark hole of my life and into a life of possibilities, opportunities, and even miracles—a life that's now filled with happiness, inner comfort, and ease that flows with the natural rhythm of life.

Like me, you can rewrite your story to have the life you've been dreaming of. Through my love and gratitude, I'd like to offer you the inspiration to harness the power of the Universe to create accelerated improvement in the direction of your dreams.

Chapter One

You Are on Purpose

Chapter One

You Are on Purpose

Believe it or not, you are on purpose. There is a reason for you to be here, in this body, in this lifetime, with the fears you have, the failures that keep you up at night, and the flaws you are constantly trying to fix. Even though it's a part of life along with all the good things, these are probably the very things you try to hide or ignore because they make you feel bad about yourself.

You convince yourself you can't have what you want because you don't even know where to begin. You believe you don't have the talent, the money, the looks, the education, or the connections. Your thinking keeps telling you there is something wrong with you or you are not good enough.

But guess what. You have it all backward! I have worked with thousands of individuals. It might surprise you to know that the majority of people believe they are flawed in some way. Even people you aspire to be like—the ones who seem to have all the confidence in the world. Many people don't feel good enough and definitely don't think they deserve to have good things happen to them. They think those people who do succeed are lucky or they have it easy.

They think that their problems are their fault or that they did something to deserve a hard life. They also believe they are the only ones suffering with the problems they have. In their minds, everyone else lives happily and trouble free.

It is only from the perspective of working with so many people that I was able to see a common thread. We *all* have problems! Many of them! I know it sounds simplistic and we are all aware that everyone has troubles, but when you are in the midst of your own drama, you tend to suppress that knowledge. You imagine that you are the only one suffering. You forget that this too shall pass. You forget that you are not alone.

Working with clients also gave me the awareness that there is a purpose for having challenges. Your challenges are actually essential to your success—to the goals that you strive to achieve. These trials and tribulations are what set you up to expand to your greatest potential. While it may not be pleasant, the problems you face are helping you develop the very skills that are required for your next step.

All of your disappointments, your hardships, and your difficulties are stepping-stones to success. They are not random. You were not dealt a bad hand when you were born. Your challenges illuminate the path to grow to your greatest potential and the opportunity to get what you want out of life.

It is the way you view your problems that is keeping you imprisoned. With so much of your attention focused on your challenges, you are unable to see the possibilities beyond them.

Many people, however, view this differently. They firmly believe these challenges are proof that life is hard and there is no way they can have the life they want. There are too many roadblocks! It's impossible because the odds are stacked against you.

But it's not the outside world that is keeping you from accomplishing your goals and being who you truly are. It is the way you view your problems that is keeping you imprisoned. With so much of your attention focused on your challenges, you are unable to see the possibilities beyond them. Do you know that the people with the greatest challenges are the ones who carry the greatest gifts?

Many of you may feel you weren't meant to have the life you desire, and it's true that our society has a smaller group of millionaires than middle-class folks. But it has nothing to do with destiny. High levels of success are available for *everyone*. It doesn't matter if it seems unlikely or even impossible. Your history doesn't matter. It doesn't matter if you think it's only for a lucky few. People are "lucky" because of the way they think. Making some slight adjustments to your thinking will help you take enormous steps in the direction of your success.

Awaken Your Gifts

The world is depending on you to awaken your gifts, to be who you came here to be, and to have a life that you love. Your challenges are not keeping you from what you desire. How you think about each challenge determines whether you are moving closer to or farther away from the things you want.

You were born with your own unique gifts and talents. They are patiently waiting to be awakened so that the *you* who shows up is exactly who is needed to complete the exquisite tapestry of life. This is *you* in your fullest expression, the *you* that influences the well-being of others just by your presence. I'm not talking about being perfect. I'm just talking about a small shift in your thinking.

You have many seemingly real reasons why your life isn't working the way you would like. And life proves to you repeatedly that your reasons are valid—in your mind, anyway. Yet there is only one thing that is truly in your way of having your heart's desire. Webster's Dictionary defines it as "the part of a person that thinks, reasons, feels, and remembers." This describes the human mind.

Your Default Setting

Your mind has been your greatest friend. It supported you in every way as you grew and matured. Having your mind in charge of your life was the perfect default setting for your early development. It helped you learn that the stove gets hot, you can get run over if you cross the street by yourself, and you should do what Mom and Dad tell you to.

However, once the mind completes its primary role, its continued function in the same way begins to limit you rather than support you. At some point along the way in your adult life, you might have questioned or become aware that there is more beyond the thinking mind. This awareness often shows up when you feel stuck or hopeless and when something happens that makes you feel desperate enough that you are willing to look beyond the confines of your comfort zone.

You get to a point where you're not achieving what you hoped for. No matter what you try, you can't seem to make things happen. Or you have worked as hard as you could and seen minimal gain for the amount of effort invested.

This is a perfect time to remember a truth that you already know deep inside: there is something far greater in charge. You may call it Source, God, Energy, or the Universe, and there are many other names for it. This is the something that created everything, absolutely *everything*—the galaxies and all the planets; oceans, lakes, and streams; trees and plants; animals and insects; and anything else you can think of, including you!

Perhaps it's time to invite your mind to step into a secondary position and allow the Greater Universal Mind to become your guide on the next part of your journey. It will unveil a world far beyond the range of the default guide you have been using until now.

Uncover the Old Programming

Before you embark on your Universe-guided quest, you may need to look at the emotional baggage you are carrying. We all have this luggage that comes from the negative and painful experiences in life. We hold on to it and even shove it up into the overhead compartment despite that fact that it weighs us down and does more harm than good.

Thinking back to childhood, most of us heard some very limiting messages, such as the following:

- We can't afford it.
- There are starving children in India.
- You will never amount to anything.
- You're worthless.
- You're stupid.
- You're going to get fat if you eat that.
- What were you thinking?
- How could you do this to me?
- You're an embarrassment to the family.
- Wait 'til your father gets home.
- You would lose your head if it weren't attached.

Re-examine all you have been told ... Dismiss what insults your soul.—Walt Whitman

Perhaps you can't recall specific hurtful words that were said to you, but you can remember what it *felt* like to grow up in your home. Maybe nothing you could do would please your parents, or you always had the feeling of being unwanted as a child. Were there times when you felt invisible? Perhaps there was no safe place, or your sibling was favored over you. Perhaps you were always picked last for the team. Perhaps there were moments of great embarrassment.

These hurtful messages create what I call a *filter* that we use for the rest of our lives. Anything that anyone says to us is heard through this filter, which means that whatever is said is not heard accurately. You've experienced this if you've ever had your buttons pushed. Notice how you overreact. It's the same as rubbing salt on your arm. It doesn't usually hurt, but if you have a cut on your arm and rub salt on it, it will *really* hurt.

Unless we do something to heal the past hurt, we will continue to view life through these filters. Undoing the hurtful messages from the past will dramatically free up your future. We can build a whole new foundation that will support your growth and expansion and help you have the life of your dreams—a life that works *for* you rather than *to* you or *against* you.

There is a reason for everything, and you are who you are, where you are, doing what you're doing, all at the right moment. You are on purpose.

The power of the Universe provides magic and miracles in life. It allows you to take enormous leaps forward in the direction you wish to go. It turns the impossible into probable and from there into inevitable, even when it doesn't make sense to your mind. You are a very valuable person in this complex world, and you have so much to offer that you haven't even begun to realize. There is a reason for you. You are on purpose.

I invite you to try the strategy below, which is a simple meditation technique you can use anytime or for any situation. It also gives you a great appreciation for the outdoors. I love it because it helps me clear my head. Then join me in chapter 2, where we take a look at the stories we tell ourselves and how they affect our lives. The law of attraction shows us how our beliefs influence what we receive.

Strategy

WALKING MINDFULLY

Meditation is a wonderful way to become present and to detach from the worries of the future as well as the past. Some people are hesitant to try meditation because they don't feel comfortable sitting down and being still. So I suggest a simple exercise: walking mindfully. It brings you to the here and now, and through nature, opens your eyes to the beauty of Source.

Choose an outdoor, peaceful place for your walk and really observe everything around you, including the color of the leaves and how the color changes when the breeze blows them. Notice the shape of the clouds and listen to the squirrels chittering to each other. This is one of my favorite discoveries that continues to support me. When I do this exercise, I notice the temperature of the breeze on my skin, the crunch of my footsteps walking on dry leaves, the sounds in the distance, the warmth of the sun on my back, and the smell of nearby blossoms. I continue to notice all of this as I walk without allowing my mind to be distracted.

This is such a powerful exercise. Your thoughts cannot be doing two things at once, and you are choosing pleasant thoughts just by experiencing your surroundings without judging. This puts your mind and your Being at ease, helps support healing, increases inner knowing, and improves your access to Universal Wisdom. It is a pathway to oneness and bliss.

If you really take this on, your life will begin to change, seemingly all on its own. And as it changes, you will begin to create from a whole new level of Being. It's like the pathway to what you want to create begins to widen. It will be easier for you to have more positive thoughts and for all the good in life to flow to you. It continues to get easier and easier.

Chapter Two

What Is Your Story?

Chapter Two

What Is Your Story?

We all have a narrative in our minds—a tale of the story of our lives. This narrative dictates how we perceive ourselves. It shapes our daily actions and influences the choices we make.

The story that you tell yourself was formed in childhood, and it is based on what you experienced, observed, and overheard, or what you may have been told. It was taken in at the level of understanding you had as a child without the ability to discern if the information was true, if it was meant for someone else, or if you simply misunderstood. This same immature story or programming still guides your life today. Once you become aware of this automatic programming, you can change it to something that positively influences your life rather than something that holds you back.

If you have a positive self-image, your story is uplifting and inspiring. It guides you toward fulfilling your purpose in life. If you have an unpleasant self-image, as I had, your story is loaded with drama and tragedy that brings you down. You may not even realize it, but these thoughts are there, integrated into your daily life. For instance, your script might say, *I'm ugly. I'm stupid. I'm lazy.* So you beat yourself up. Lacking self-confidence, you doubt your ability to achieve your goals, and the voice inside your head says, *I'll never find love. I'll never be happy. I'll never get what I want out of life.* Or *Why me? Why do the good things always happen to other people?*

What is your story? Is it filled with self-defeating thoughts? If so, you are more likely to feel depressed and experience helplessness and hopelessness. You may be unable to shake the feeling that nothing you do ever works, so why even try. This is because thoughts like *I can't do this* or *I'll never succeed* condition you to believe that you can't achieve your goals in life, you can't get ahead, and you'll never be happy. Failure becomes a self-fulfilling prophecy.

Fortunately, there is a solution: you can use simple techniques to make powerful life changes and rewrite the story of your life to a life-affirming, self-enhancing script by changing your thoughts from unpleasant to positive, as I did. When you do, you too will become the master of your own life and change it so you can experience an inner sense of peace, plenty of energy, and high productivity. You'll also see an increase in confidence and the ability to meet your goals as you start living in the natural rhythm and flow of life. And most importantly, you'll experience more happiness.

The Law of Attraction

Imagine yourself right now lying on a beach with the sun pouring down on you and the relaxing sound of the waves in your ears. What joy! What freedom! Can you feel it? Can you feel the warmth of the sun and the sound of the waves?

What gives our thoughts so much power? Our thoughts resonate with an energy, a vibrational level that we might interpret as either positive or negative. At any moment in time, the level at which we vibrate attracts more of that same vibration to us. I'm going to repeat that: the level at which we vibrate attracts more of that same vibration to us. That means that whatever you are experiencing right now emotionally, you are attracting more of the same emotions, situations, and things of a similar vibration to you.

If you are wallowing in self-pity or jealousy or anger about not having enough, you are drawing more of that to your life right now and every day until something changes. This book may provide the "something" to make those changes.

At any moment in time, the level at which we vibrate attracts more of that same vibration to us.

When you live a miraculous life, you will expect that good things are always coming your way, even though you may not see proof of it yet and even when it seems that the opposite is true. When that happens, your thoughts and your responses to the situations in life will be of a much higher vibration. Your body and your Being will feel more at ease, and the possibilities and opportunities in life will begin to flow to you freely. This will enable you to live in the natural rhythm and flow of the Universe and begin to live a miraculous life.

You'll be surprised at how much the world around you can change in an instant when you change the way you look at it. The old saying "It's all in your head" is actually true! That's where changing your life starts—in your head and in your heart. When your thinking matches your vibration, which is the frequency of your energy, outside forces will align with what you desire, according to the inspirational Abraham-Hicks, a spirit guide group that speaks through Esther Hicks,

Dale Carnegie, a highly-respected lecturer and author in the early 1900s, said that your happiness comes from your thoughts—not from the material goods you have, or who you know, or who you are. It all comes down to what you're thinking.

It Just Waits for Your Command

If you were building a house, you wouldn't go to a contractor and just ask him to build a house. You might get a one-room shack! There would be a lot of things to consider. How many square feet? What style of construction? Do you want brick? Stucco? Wood siding? One story or two? How many bedrooms? What do you want the kitchen to be like? Do you want big windows or more privacy? How big would the lot be? You would give the contractor directions to create the perfect home for you.

The Invisible Power is like the contractor. It is simply waiting for you to tell it what you want. What you have been telling the Power or Creator up until this point is what you see going on in your life right now. You have allowed your default thinking to determine what your life should look like. You do this every day through your thoughts and emotions. It just takes small shifts to make big differences. Instead, what most people do is take more classes, work longer hours, network more, scramble to make a living, etc.

I'm not suggesting that you change your thinking and then sit on the sofa all day watching soap operas. However, changing your thinking as well as your story is the single most powerful and essential thing you can do to change the circumstances of your life. In addition, you will be taking some action, but it's probably not as difficult as what you are already doing.

Three Steps to Changing Your Thinking

Your thoughts are incredibly powerful. The old saying about how the mind can move mountains is true. While our thoughts can keep us inert, causing depression and hopelessness, they can also inspire us to move and take action to make our dreams come true. So how do you change what you think? How do you start living a life of miracles? How do you get to that place of inner contentment? You must build your support, prepare yourself for the unexpected, and expect phenomenal things to happen.

Find a thought that feels better. It's a simple choice.

Step 1: Your Foundation

First, you build a foundation. Remember I talked about the facade I had built that crumbled? When the facade was gone, I had to start building my foundation, my support. Part of constructing this foundation was learning to take charge of my mind so I could stop creating unwanted situations and experiences and begin to attract more of what I wanted in life. It's important at this stage to change your thinking habits that involve judgment and negativity. Find a thought that feels better. It's a simple choice.

Break the habit of being envious of others. Envy creates more lack in your life, which is the opposite of what you want. When you are envious, you put your attention on what you don't have, thereby creating more situations and experiences in the future that make you resentful. It is a never-ending cycle of the current state you are in. Besides, if you're worried that someone is better-looking, more talented, or has a better life, you are wasting time that could be spent working toward your own goals. Comparing yourself to others only serves to devalue your sense of self. As Mark Twain said, "Comparison is the death of joy."

Your foundation should include lots of positive reinforcement. Avoid reacting to situations with quick and negative assumptions. Don't give too much attention to those dramatic thoughts that lead you to assume the worst in every scenario. Surround yourself with positive people who are open to possibilities. Really give some thought to the people you spend time with. You *will* become more like them. Wherever they are vibrationally, your vibration will want to match theirs automatically. If they are happy, successful people, you are likely to become happier and more successful. If they are always complaining and constantly surrounded by drama, you will begin to attract more of that into your life. Not what you want!

Step 2: Miracle Preparation

Next, you must prepare your mind for miracles. This is simple once you have started building your foundation and have taken charge of your mind. You can't expect to be open to new possibilities when your mind is busy telling you what you can't do and what won't work. As you train your brain to avoid negative thoughts, you open it to accept things that may seem impossible and defy all logic.

Having an open mind and taking action are essential. At first, a goal or desire may seem out of reach. But those doubts and resistance will work against you no matter how much you want something. You must believe that you deserve what you want and that you will get what you are asking for. By being open to abundance as you take action, your positive mind can increase the possibilities. When you are truly open to them, miracles do indeed happen.

Step 3: Miracle Expectation

The third step is to *expect* miracles to happen. This is the natural outcome of steps 1 and 2. It's our natural way of being, and it is truly this simple! This joyful anticipation really makes wonderful things happen in life.

Anticipation is a key word here. Miracles are just waiting for you to be ready to receive them. It doesn't matter who you are or how difficult your life has been up to this point—the miracles that are yours are just waiting for you to be ready for them.

Take a look at this chapter's strategy for stopping negative thoughts and consider how quickly your emotions can move through your body and how easy it is to attach to the negative thoughts. In the next chapter, I'll delve deeper into the thought process. You'll be amazed at how self-defeating thoughts not only make a situation worse but attract more of the same problems.

Strategy

STOPPING YOUR NEGATIVE THOUGHTS

Become aware of what your mind is doing. Notice your fearful thoughts, judgments, complaints, etc. We all live on autopilot, and these unpleasant thinking habits are where most people spend their time. The mind just loves to be in charge. It has been running your life until this moment.

Allowing your mind to continue in this manner will bring more of what you have right now. If you want something better, it is time to take control of your thinking and stop any negative thought as soon as you notice it. Do this before your mind takes the thought and creates a lot of drama and other thoughts around it.

Neuroscience explains this process. The average time it takes for an emotion to move through the nervous system and body is ninety seconds. After that, we need thoughts to keep the emotion rolling. In other words, our own inner dialogue is what keeps us locked into painful emotional states like anxiety, fear, sadness, depression, or rage.

Remember that no matter what kind of emotion the thought evokes—whether it's fear, disappointment, self-criticism, or sadness—it's not fact. It's just a thought.

Chapter Three

Whether You Think You Can or Can't

Chapter Three

Whether You Think You Can or Can't

On average, you have 70,000 thoughts per day. If you have a stressful life or a lot of anxiety, you likely have even more thoughts per day, and most of the thoughts are unpleasant or at least less than neutral.

What does your inner voice usually say to you? What is it telling you about yourself? Is it telling you how loved and appreciated you are, what great things you are doing with your life, and how deserving you are of wonderful things? Are your thoughts telling you that life is safe and good and even more good things are coming your way? Do you feel confident that you are making wise choices?

Or is your inner narrative one that makes you feel bad about yourself? Maybe it tells you things like the following:

- "You are too fat."
- "You could never afford to buy the home of your dreams."
- "Your body will never heal."
- "Your life will never improve."
- "You'll never find a perfect relationship."
- "You don't deserve something better in life."
- "No one can be trusted."
- "Changing your situation is hopeless."
- "You should have done things differently."
- "If only you could just disappear."

Stop complaining! You attract more things to complain about whenever you are focused on something you don't like.

If this self-defeating dialogue sounds like your story, it's creating unwanted emotions and feelings in your body and Being that will attract more situations at that same level. By letting these conversations continue, you are creating fertile ground for more weeds in your life. That's not what you want to be doing if you want your life to improve. And you can change this!

Neuroscience Has Your Back

You can change your story to a positive and life-affirming one that raises your personal vibration and prepares your foundation for miracles. You can actually change your past experiences of sadness, guilt, hopelessness, lack of confidence, and difficult situations that left you fearful and untrusting. You can change anything that has challenged you and made your life difficult up until now. You can improve your life by learning to change how you respond to these thoughts and experiences. Neuroscience, which deals with the function of your brain and nervous system, backs this up.

Neuroscience has a saying: "Neurons that fire together, wire together." This means that the more you think about certain experiences, the stronger the memory and the more easily activated the related feelings become. If those thoughts are negative, feeding them will keep them in the loop. This is what we do by default.

For example, let's say a young girl shows her mother the beautiful paper flowers she made for her mother's birthday. Her mother says they're lovely but throws them in the garbage. The emotional pain of rejection may become linked with any number of thoughts or beliefs:

- I'm not loved.
- I'm not worth her time.
- I don't make pretty things.
- It's not safe to expect to be loved.
- I'm not important to her.
- I hate her.

The more the child gets this response from her mother—or even imagines getting this response—the greater the need for the mother's attention and interest. This becomes paired with the belief that she will be refused and the accompanying feelings of fear, hurt, anger, and shame. Years later, she may hesitate to even try to produce something creative, expecting rejection or disinterest. If she does make an effort and the other person so much as pauses or looks distracted, the old feelings instantly take over. She downplays her need for approval, attention, interest, or caring. She apologizes, becomes enraged, or withdraws inward, denying her feelings altogether.

People spend years in talk therapy trying to break through these repetitive, destructive emotional patterns. Yet research shows that you can change self-defeating chatter from your neurocircuits with the right strategies. You can supercharge changes in your life by using powerful techniques to change your thoughts and anything else in your life.

Replacing Your Thoughts

It was difficult for me to simply stop my thoughts, but I learned how to replace them with more useful ones. I used to have terrible, obsessive, fearful thoughts that controlled my life, and this exercise was the most doable for me. My upsetting thoughts were just too overpowering to simply quiet my mind; the most effective solution was to replace the thoughts.

Most people are not used to having nothing going on in their minds, so stopping their thoughts feels foreign. However, we can replace unwanted thoughts with something more pleasant. The substitute thought doesn't even need to be related to or even the opposite of the unpleasant thought. For example, let's say you are beating yourself up for something you said to a friend. Replacing the thought by imagining that you hadn't said what you said isn't going to make sense to you, and your mind won't believe it. So you will create more mind chatter about how stupid this exercise is and how this won't work.

Instead, try replacing the thought with a wonderful memory, a favorite image of one of your animals, or something you are looking forward to doing. You can also use a prayer or a mantra or anything that resonates with you. Anything that is pleasant and of a higher vibration will distract your mind from taking on the unpleasant thought and weaving an entire story about it. This process will immediately raise your vibration by focusing your attention on something positive.

Think about how the sun is trickling in through the blinds and you can see the speckles of dust floating in and out of the light. Notice how the light is slowly taking away more and more of the shadows. Laugh as your dog wriggles around on the rug, trying to find the spot most in contact with a sunbeam.

Live life as if everything is rigged in your favor.—Rumi

I know this might sound a little tedious, but here's why it works. According to researcher Benjamin Libet, the part of the brain responsible for movement activates a quarter second before we become aware of our intention to move. Another quarter second passes before the movement begins. So you have a quarter second to stop these looping thoughts and accompanying unpleasant emotions.

Say you've been obsessing about taking a bite of chocolate cake. During the space between the impulse (the desire for the cake) and the action (grabbing a slice) lies choice. If you catch your thoughts in the "magic quarter-second," as author Tara Bennett-Goleman named it, and refocus your attention, you can interrupt the compulsive thinking that fuels anxiety and other painful emotions. In this way, you can replace an unnecessary defensive judgment with a more patient and compassionate approach in the present moment.

I encourage you to try this chapter's strategy of distracting yourself from unproductive thoughts. Sometimes we all just need a break. In the next chapter, we'll take a look at how your dreams may not be so impossible. You may not even be aware of those deep desires that are waiting to evolve.

Strategy

DISTRACTION CAN BE A GOOD THING

Distraction is a helpful tool whenever your mind is caught up in negative thinking. It's important to do whatever it takes to interrupt these thoughts. It's too difficult to quiet your mind when you are struggling with this, so distraction is an ideal method. Do anything that requires your full attention and is enjoyable. It can be shooting baskets, doing target practice—anything that uses focus. Or try cooking something that requires following a recipe or building something that requires using instructions and demands all your focus.

This is especially useful when you're overwhelmed with negative thoughts and feel like you have too many problems to deal with. Take time out to enjoy something that gives your mind a break, and then when you go back to the issues, they may not seem as difficult. You'll have a fresh perspective.

Chapter Four

Who Do You Think You Are?

Chapter Four

Who Do You Think You Are?

We all have hidden fears about what we deserve in life. They may be hidden deep inside on your most confident days, but the underlying question you constantly ask yourself is, *Who am I to have what I want?* Most people have a sense of being unworthy or undeserving even if they are unaware of it. This lack of self-worth hinders your ability to receive, which means your dreams will forever remain dreams and not become your reality.

Whatever your career, family situation, or aspirations, you may wonder why you would be so blessed or why in the world your goals would ever be met. *Who am I to be successful? Who am I to deserve a loving relationship? Who am I to be an author, a public speaker, a teacher, a leader, a parent?*

Many people have enormous dreams of doing something really big. Yet few people ever achieve those dreams. Most are too embarrassed to even admit what their dreams are, or they limit their dreams to what they think they can have, not what they really want. Some people won't even go there. They won't allow themselves to have a big dream.

I have a secret to share with you. Do you know that your deepest desires are not coming from your ego? Your longing for enormous success is not just a frivolous wish. When you have a deep, heartfelt desire, it is actually your soul calling.

This is why you have the desire. I want you to really take in what this means. The true desire you feel is an invitation from your soul to manifest your desire into reality. It also means that you already have what it takes to make it a reality even if it seems impossible from where you are right now. You would not have this dream if you weren't given the invitation to make it a reality in your life. You were meant to have it as an avenue of expression of the Divine.

> *When you have a deep, heartfelt desire, it is actually your soul calling.*

This understanding was one of the single most important pieces of information for me. It gave me the permission I needed to have ridiculously lofty hopes and dreams—and to feel worthy of attaining them. The book *You Squared* by Price Pritchett begins with a quote from Heraclitus that I love: "If you do not expect it, you will not find the unexpected."

As we journey together in this life, let's learn to expect the unexpected. Let's dare to dream big and fully expect our dreams to become a reality.

Your Heartfelt Desire

What is it that you want? What is your heartfelt desire? If you had a magic wand, what would your life be like?

A heartfelt desire sometimes feels so big that it's embarrassing to even mention to anyone. And you don't have to. You can keep this to yourself if you choose. There is one teaching that suggests saying your desire out loud leaks energy and weakens your ability to achieve it. Another teaching suggests letting a group know your dream so that they can support and hold space for you to help you accomplish your goal.

What I have found is that sharing your dream with people who support and believe in possibilities keeps you on track, which helps manifestation happen faster. Talking about your dream with people who are not aware of the magic of life and spiritual principles works against you and creates enough doubt to halt your dream.

What Do You Really Want?

The first step in this journey is to clarify what it is you really want. You might answer that you could use a new car or you have been wanting to remodel your kitchen. That isn't what I mean. What would make your heart sing? What is your heartfelt desire? Maybe it's so big that it's buried deep inside your subconscious where it rarely surfaces. Maybe you were taught that you can't have it, so you've never even really considered it.

Give yourself permission. Take a moment now to form in your mind what it is you really want, not just what you think you can have. This is an important difference. What is your deep desire, even if it sounds silly to you and you know that there is no way you could ever have it? What would that desire be—to be a public speaker, win an Oscar, earn a higher education? Maybe your desire is to become a parent, help by counseling others, or have a loving and intimate relationship. Do you want to travel around the world, climb Mount Everest, or sip wine at an Italian sidewalk café?

When you have an idea or a picture in your mind of what you really, really would love to have, write it down. You will want to have your dream in writing so that it can serve as a reminder and stay at the forefront of your mind. I suggest writing it on a piece of paper that you will see often or enter it into your phone or computer so you'll be reminded of it.

Adding Fuel to Your Dream

Defining your goal or dream is the first step. However, we also want to add fuel to your aspirations. Without fuel, your dream will remain a dream and not come to fruition.

To fuel your dream, you will want to read your goal a minimum of twice a day and as often as possible. You might find you want to polish your statement so it is really a match for the outcome you desire. It's just fine to do that. Visualize, imagine, and pretend—whatever it takes to see your future in a positive way.

What is important when you read your goal is to imagine your life as if your dream has already come true. How would you feel? See yourself walking into your new home. What does the doorknob look like? Does the door have a window or a decorative knocker? What color is it painted, or is it stained? What is the first thing you notice when you open the door? Get in touch with what it would be like. The feeling is essential. Otherwise, reading your goal is meaningless.

> ***Visualize, imagine, and pretend—whatever it takes to see your future in a positive way.***

Emotion is key. Your ability to really feel your dream as if it were already true will speed its fruition. Believe in possibilities! Believe in your dream even when your current reality does not reflect what you desire. This is where the Universe takes over. It's not necessary to be concerned with *how* it will happen; in fact, if you know how, your dream is not big enough. Your role is not to know how. Your only focus is the end result. Everything else will fall into place.

Figure out what your true passion is and hand your dream over to a Higher Power to handle. This is where trust comes in. Trust that life is working on your behalf. It's being handled *for* you, not by you. This is the key piece. It would not be possible to attain your dream if you had to figure it out by yourself. Your excited anticipation and certainty of your goal will fuel the momentum of the expected outcome.

Visualization—See it in Your Mind's Eye

Your imagination is a powerful resource that you can use to create your own world. Visualization is a fantastic tool to use when working to acquire your dreams.

What You See Is Truly What You Get

Take a minute to visualize or imagine your goal, your dream, or the result you are hoping for. See the details in your mind.

Many years ago, I was looking for a solid, loving relationship. I used my imagination to visualize the perfect partner for me. I never saw his face, but I would imagine the two of us walking hand in hand facing away from me as the viewer. Not only did I end up with the man that I imagined, I ended up owning the property in my visualization as well.

Imagine how you would feel if your dream had already come true. Use your creativity to visualize it.

Use Props

You can use a dream board or affirmation cards to help your mind focus on a concept or goal. When you use these kinds of tools, you'll want to do so with a sense of enjoyment. Create these from a place of playfulness and fun. If the suggestion or the activity of making visual aids sounds like a chore, however, this won't work for you.

Trust the Universe to Take Care of the "How"

After you feel you are pretty good at seeing that picture of success, it's okay to relax and go with the flow. The Universe knows what you desire and has a way of lighting up the path to that success. Even if you have no clue about how to get to where you want to be, don't stress; that will be taken care of naturally.

Your Emotions Will Lead the Way

What's even more important than "seeing" what you want is feeling what you want. Using imagination or visualization needs to be fun and open-ended, meaning that there isn't a right or wrong way. It is pure desire running through you. The details might shift or become a little more defined, but the overall feeling is one of joy and delight.

I suppose one of the few rules would be if your visualization required a certain person to be part of it or if you were including any steps to get to the outcome you desire. But that would shut down the flow. It is only the end result you want to focus on— and how it would feel when it had already come true.

Don't Be the Fly

Society has taught us that if we work hard, we will be rewarded. But that is true only to a certain extent. You may get to a point where the rewards are definitely not worth the amount of work you've been putting in. You don't seem to be gaining anything but frustration and fatigue. You may have that underlying thought that says you aren't working hard enough, but working even harder to achieve a goal is not the solution.

At the beginning of *You Squared*, Price Pritchett describes his observation of a fly that uses up the last of its energy trying to reach the outdoors by flying through the glass of a windowpane. No matter how hard it tries, it can never break through the glass and succeed. The fly is doomed to exhaust all of its energy and die on the windowsill.

Just a few feet away, there is an open door. The fly could have spent very little of its precious energy and easily reached the outside world that it sought. But the fly was too locked into this one idea that this particular route seemed to be the only way to succeed.

A good work ethic is important, but sometimes instead of working harder, you need to work smarter—or even just find a different avenue or way of doing things. Trying harder at the same thing you've been doing is, at best, not the solution to your success. At worst, it is a major part of the problem. By continuing to do things the same way, like the fly ramming its body into the windowpane, you are decreasing the effectiveness of all your hard work.

In the next chapter, we will explore the endless possibilities that come along when we are open to adventure. Sometimes we fight the natural order of things instead of going with the flow. First, I would like to offer you the strategy for this chapter, which will help you to be open to everything wonderful that the Universe is offering.

Strategy

JUST SAY YES

This exercise may seem overly simplistic, yet it is one of the most powerful that I have discovered. The word *yes* is absolutely magical! It is like a key that unlocks the power of the Universe and the world of manifestation. Repeating the word *yes* as part of a walking meditation has had a profound effect on my frame of mind, my state of Being, and my ability to access the natural rhythm and flow of life. It is so simple, and yet it produces extraordinary results.

This is all you need to do to access the power that the word *yes* provides. Start with a "walking mindfully" exercise (see chapter 1). If you have the opportunity to walk where there are few distractions, even better. Become aware of your surroundings and be completely present. Notice the sounds and the smells. Notice the temperature on your skin.

Once you are settled into your surroundings, use the word *yes* as part of a mantra or a phrase that you will be repeating. I used a variety of phrases, usually beginning with, "Yes to life." It's my personal favorite. You can make up any phrases that are a match for you. Possibilities include the following:

- yes to love
- yes to inner peace
- yes to vibrancy
- yes to a strong body
- yes to forgiveness
- yes to balance
- yes to kindness

- yes to giving
- yes to receiving
- yes to possibilities
- yes to miracles

Chapter Five
Surrender to the Universe

Chapter Five

Surrender to the Universe

Life brings all kinds of experiences, wanted and unwanted. We do our best to consciously create an easier life. We monitor our thoughts. We focus on the positive. We use tools and techniques to make our lives better.

Perhaps you use energy work, or you enjoy using affirmations. You may like to listen to inspirational teachers or read uplifting books. All of these things help raise your vibration so you can attract more pleasant experiences into your life.

And still, life happens. It happens to all of us. There are always going to be ups and downs as well as some very trying experiences, but we can choose how we are going to respond to these circumstances when they happen.

Surrender + Trust + Gratitude = Serenity

A spiritual teacher once told me that everything in life has a purpose. Anything that happens to you, whether it seems good or bad, is happening *for* you. All of it—it's a gift. I know it's hard to grasp that idea, because we have all experienced some rough moments in life. However, even the most challenging problems are here to serve you and help you grow. These hard times in life usually make us grow very rapidly.

Difficult experiences only seem so because of how we perceive them. How you view the situation determines how easy or hard it feels.

This makes a big difference in how we react to the situation and what steps we take next. Keep in mind this equation: Surrender + Trust + Gratitude = Serenity.

Trust the Process

The harder we fight what the Universe is trying to give us, the more difficult the experience will be and the longer the difficulty will last. You aren't weak or a failure if you choose to let the natural order of things run its course; in fact, it takes courage to stop struggling. Whenever possible, choose acceptance instead of resistance and find something to be grateful for. Trust strengthens, doubt weakens. I have discovered that the secret to nearly instant transformation is in truly trusting the process of life. Genuine surrender to a Higher Power invites miracles into your life.

Trust strengthens, doubt weakens.

We all tend to live life doing the opposite of acceptance and surrender. This is evident every time we want something we don't have or when we try to control things because we want the outcome to look a certain way. We are in a state of resistance and are actually pushing the very things we want further away. One quick method for moving out of resistance is to use energy work to address any items in the way. There are additional ways to move toward a happier life, such as changing your thoughts, reading inspirational books, meditating, and surrounding yourself with positive people.

Match Your Vibration

Matching the vibration of your dream makes it come so much faster. Your emotional state shows you what you are bringing into your life right now. If it's of a low vibration, do something to kick it up a notch.

Go outside, call a friend, get up and stretch, listen to an inspirational recording, focus on a favorite inspirational quote and feel the feeling of it, or look at a favorite photo of your dog and feel your connection. What you attract is always a vibrational match to your emotions. If you don't like how your life is going, change how you feel.

It's not always easy to switch to a positive vibration, especially if you've been in a low one for any amount of time. Your vibration will rise much more quickly if you notice unwanted thoughts as soon as they occur. Work on allowing instead of pushing for things to happen. Work at the action part a little less; imagine your goals and dreams more. Feel as if it is already true.

We are often faced with tasks we don't want to do or decisions we don't want to make. It can be very confusing when you are trying to decide what to do to achieve your dreams. But there is your problem. The magic is in the believing and imagining, not in the doing. Take action only when you are inspired to do so. Forced action stops or delays positive manifestation. It's also important to constantly program positive information into your mind. Listen to inspirational recordings when driving or getting ready in the morning.

Are You Open to Adventure?

Exciting things happen when you live in the natural rhythm and flow of life. Many years ago, I was leading a workshop at the local health care district, and afterward I met a friend for dinner. I was in a great mood, all pumped after leading this workshop and really looking forward to spending time with my friend. So there I was, all dressed up. As I walked into the restaurant in my elegant clothes and high heels, I slipped and fell on the wet tile floor. Now this was *not* a graceful fall. My legs shot out from under me, throwing my body into the air before I landed flat on my back.

Now usually, in a situation like this, I would have been incredibly embarrassed. I mean, here I was, decked out to the max, making a complete fool of myself! I would normally wonder if I had broken something—or even worse, if someone saw the accident. All of these are low-vibrational thoughts. Instead, the only thought that went through my mind was, *I wonder what adventure this will bring?* There was no resistance, no embarrassment, no alarming concern about what people might think, and no wishing it had been any different from what it was. Just complete acceptance.

Little did I know where this adventure would lead; I'll share that you in chapter 6. For now, I want you to realize that the key to achieving your goals is to allow the natural order of things. Find the rhythm of your life through acceptance and surrender.

The Universe Is Listening

There are many ways you can tell that the Universe is listening. It may communicate through nature. You feel a lift of spirits when a butterfly flutters around your head or you watch the fireflies as the sun is setting. When you are looking for the signs, a cardinal may be singing just for you or a squirrel may remind you to have fun and be silly. You might find items with messages from the Universe, like pennies in unexpected places or feathers along your path.

Messages or encouragement may come in the form of repeating numbers or a song that comes on the radio and seems to resonate within you. If you look around, you'll see messages in the billboards or on the tire cover of a Jeep Wrangler that reads, "Life is good."

Events that happen just when you need them to could be synchronicity or meaningful coincidences. For instance, just as your savings run dry, you find a job. Or you meet a stranger who has the perfect words to bring you back into focus. Have you ever known a person who seems to be popping into your life more often? Did that person become your significant other or bring something valuable to your life?

The Universe offers lots of support in ways you don't even recognize. You can improve the quality of your life just by becoming aware and appreciating these special moments and synchronicities. Let's do a process on acceptance with this image that has been energized. This will help you move more easily into acceptance so you are no longer resisting the natural flow of the Universe.

In the next chapter, I explain how your transformation is entirely possible even though it may seem unbelievable. It's not only a leap of faith; it can be a huge jump!

Strategy

FOCUS ON ACCEPTANCE

Settle down on the floor or on a chair—anywhere comfortable. As you look at this picture, imagine a brilliant, sparkling beam of white light between the image and the center of your forehead. Feel the essence of it and relax. Focus on the image for approximately a minute. Breathe in the word *acceptance*.

Chapter Six
Explosive Jumps—Taking Quantum Leaps

Chapter Six

Explosive Jumps—Taking Quantum Leaps

We are told to be patient when it comes to getting what we want. We are led to believe that nothing is going to get us to our goals but small, incremental steps. Society tells us it's a process. One day at a time. Put one foot in front of the other. But there is another way to realize your dreams if you are open to the wonders of the Universe and willing to change how you see it.

Some scientists explain the Universe through quantum physics, which is the study of the process of atoms, protons, and all that fun stuff. At the fundamental level, a quantum leap is the irregular change as the electron in a molecule or atom goes from one energy level to another. At a relatable level, our world would be incredibly different if it wasn't for quantum physics, especially in the computer technology industry.

At the microscopic level, a quantum leap is a colossal change that happens suddenly. The atoms and protons don't take it one step at a time. When it's time for a change, they practically explode into the next energy state without any effort.

It boggles the mind to think that if particles do this and we're made up of this stuff, perhaps we as human beings can make these explosive jumps to achieve our goals. We may have to redefine how we see the Universe, but yes, we have the capability—as well as many opportunities to take quantum leaps in our lives.

Price Pritchett agrees and says you don't have to settle for limited steps toward what you want when you can take quantum leaps. We've been taught that slow and steady wins the race. But having to take gradual steps toward a dream is a misconception.

Change in Behavior

A quantum leap requires an abrupt change in behavior. According to Abraham-Hicks, if you're constantly trying to go upstream against the current, try going with the flow. You'll get better results if you use finesse instead of effort. Even the slightest shift in thinking will make an enormous change in your reality.

It's easy to understand why the fly keeps banging into the window to get out. That's what he knows to do, and it has worked in the past—probably with an open window. We do the same thing by going back to the basics because we've been successful there before. And it's especially tempting to do so when we're really good at what we do. But that doesn't mean we should keep doing it, according to Price Pritchett. In fact, doing something that you excel at can actually be detrimental to achieving your dream if it's not in alignment with who you are.

You must do something new even though it may seem to go against every fiber of your Being. Old habits are hard to break, and it's more comfortable to stay with the familiar, however painful or ineffective.

Even the slightest shift in thinking will make an enormous change in your reality.

This new approach will be less demanding of your energy and emotions but will most likely seem very strange to you at first. An explosive jump will put you far beyond the next logical step, and although that sounds great on the surface, we are not conditioned for such radical change, even if it is for our benefit. We've been taught that things like this don't happen that easily. That it's not possible. Pritchett explains this concept in mathematical terms: instead of adding small steps, the quantum leap multiplies the payoffs you will receive.

Trying to wrap your mind around the idea that things can happen in your life beyond what you are expecting right now in such an explosive manner may be difficult. But even though it doesn't make any sense, it does happen in the scientific processes. If it happens with particles, it can happen to you. It happened to me when I experienced a spontaneous healing many years ago. The spontaneous healing was a quantum leap. The impossible happened.

Spontaneous Healing

After I took that nasty fall at the restaurant, my life changed quite dramatically. The next morning, when I tried to get out of bed, I found my leg wouldn't hold my weight, and I immediately fell to the floor in pain. I discovered that my leg would no longer stay in the hip socket. If I tried to walk normally, it would give out, and I would fall to the ground once again in excruciating pain. What was I going to do? How dramatically would my life change?

Before the fall, I had been very active. But in an instant, everything changed. My life became very limited. I could no longer walk my dogs or explore the acres of orchards where we lived. If I wanted to walk anywhere, I had to pull on my pant leg to propel my leg forward in order to take each step. There would be no more putting my hands in my pockets if I was cold. I needed to be ready to catch myself when I fell, which happened often.

In an instant, everything changed. My life became very limited. I could no longer walk my dogs or explore the acres of orchards.

I didn't have insurance at the time, so there was no way for me to have hip replacement surgery or whatever would have been needed to fix the problem. Yet part of me was okay with all of this. It was just the way it was, and I focused on acceptance. Limited mobility simply became a new way of living. When my husband was building my healing studio, I asked him to be sure the doorway was wide enough for a wheelchair, because I felt I was going to need one in the near future.

Nearly a year later, my family was planning a vacation to San Francisco. I secretly dreaded the thought of going. If you know anything about San Francisco, you know there is a *lot* of walking, getting into and out of trolleys, and more walking. I didn't talk to anyone about it, but I couldn't see a way I would be able to go without ruining the vacation for everyone else. I was at a loss as to what to do.

I was so upset inside, and as the time to leave for vacation grew closer, I only became more anxious. There was absolutely nothing I could do to fix this situation. Staying home wasn't an option; my family would be upset. Staying in the hotel room wasn't an option; they wouldn't want to leave me behind. In desperation, the only thing I could think of to do was to turn my worry over to a Higher Power.

I remember standing in the corner of my dining room, sincerely pouring out my heart to Source. Turning over my concerns to a Higher Power allowed me to at least let go of the worry, and I found I was able to stop thinking about my problem. I felt like it was being handled, and I could let it go.

A few days later, I was sitting at my desk doing a phone session with a client when all of a sudden, I felt a very strong vibration in my leg. Of course I didn't mention anything to the client, and I continued with the session until it ended, even though I was so curious about what had taken place. When I stood up from my chair, I discovered that somehow my leg was strong and it no longer came out of the hip socket. I walked out of my office with a normal gait, with no pain and no falling.

My leg was completely healed. I could walk my dogs and climb stairs again. I could put my hands in my pockets. And I enjoyed every moment of our family vacation to San Francisco, walking up and down hills and jumping on trolleys. What a miracle! I have been walking normally ever since.

Beyond Common Sense

We've all been taught to use common sense. Your parents most likely told you to use the brains God gave you. But I'm inviting you to throw caution to the wind and be open to monumental change. I'm asking you to think beyond what common sense would normally allow.

If you're thinking that it's impossible to get from point A to point Z without stopping anywhere in between, let that kind of common sense go and trust in the Universe. Focus on a clear picture of what it is you want. In your mind, seek out the mental image of your desired outcome.

Once you have a strong image in your head, imagine where your quantum leap will take you. Where will you land? Visualize your arrival. This will set the course for your explosive jump, even if you have no idea how this will happen.

The solutions will begin to appear. Answers will come to you. The hidden skills and talents deep inside of you will begin to develop. And you'll experience great stages of growth.

Suspend Belief

You will find that your greatest obstacle to success is doubt. Doubt can be a major roadblock to success because it brings the fear of failure, of not being good enough, of being unlovable, and of being unworthy. Doubt brings mistrust, which keeps us from surrendering to the Universe.

Notice when those kinds of pessimistic thoughts appear and suspend your old beliefs. I suggest acting as if your success is for certain. I'm not recommending that you go out and buy a new car or go into debt. I'm suggesting that the story you tell yourself is one of enormous success. Allow that feeling of success to permeate every cell of your Being and grow within you. Think of who you would call to share the news of your success. What would you say to them? How would you celebrate? How would it feel inside?

The End Result

It's so important to focus on the end result rather than on the "how." If you obsess over how in the world this is all going to happen, you will never get to the desired goal. You don't have to know how you're going to get there, but you do need to know where you want to go. The key is not to get in the way. If you know the steps needed to attain your dream, your dream is limiting and not reflecting your true potential. By organizing your journey, you are telling the Universe that you can do it on your own, and you don't want any assistance.

The "how" would be more like a plan of how to attain what you want: *I'll ask my wealthy uncle for a loan. I'll visualize my jewelry sales going up to help support the payments.* This is a plan of how a person thinks it will happen. Planning like this is a message to the Universe that you don't need the help of a Higher Power—you can do this on your own. It's the exact opposite of what you want. Focus on the end result and allow the Universe to figure out how to make it happen.

For example, say your dream is to move near the ocean. At first, you have visions of lounging on the deck of your beach house, watching the crash of the waves and soaking in the sun. But then you start to wonder how it could possibly happen. You remember that you are barely staying afloat financially where you are, and it costs an incredible amount of money to move your entire household to a new location. As you focus on how to make this move happen and forget that beach-house fantasy, the Universe brings you what you are focused on. While you're worried about renting a U-Haul trailer, your car breaks down. When you constantly worry about finding a cheap place to live at the beach, your rent goes up. You don't think you'll be able to find a decent job in your new location, and your present job cuts your hours.

Trust and focus only on the outcome. Leave the "how" up to the Universe to handle for you. The Universe knows far more than you do.

You don't need a plan or a map. You can make it up as you go. You don't need a guide or any kind of GPS; you just need to focus on the target and your end goal. Action will move the energy in the direction it needs to go, but it's important to visualize where you're going to land.

A quantum leap is not something you have to work at to create. It's a move you're already prepared to make. You just haven't done it yet. According to Pritchett, this explosive jump can't be forced. You just have to let it happen—and make sure you're not in the way.

You are choosing the direction and providing the fuel with your vision held in excited anticipation. Source takes over from there. It's so simple, it boggles the mind!

Rely on Unseen Forces

Just because you don't see proof of something doesn't mean it doesn't exist, according to Carl Sagan. It's important to open yourself up to the unseen forces of the Universe.

A quantum leap isn't something you can do on your own. A quantum leap relies on unseen forces, such as God or Source. The magic of life is just waiting for you to call on it. Its purpose is to love, support, and assist you in having what you want. You just need to remember that it is your cherished partner, and it's here to serve you.

These unseen forces often operate through your subconscious mind, mental imagery, beliefs, and intuition. What you may think of as luck is really about thinking in a certain way. It's all about allowing what you want to flow into your life. The only reason you don't have what you want is because you are resisting it with your thoughts and beliefs.

Although you are clearly asking for that new job or relationship, you are focused on your doubts that it will happen. When your thinking is in alignment with what you want, your vibration will attract exactly that.

This is why working with the unconscious mind through the use of hypnosis or meditation can be so powerful in aligning your belief system with the miracles you want to attract. Otherwise, your mind works against you and not with you.

You might have a flash of inspiration during a moment of solitude. A creative solution to a problem may come to you in a dream. You may get an inspirational idea while you're visualizing your goal. Somehow what you need just seems to appear by coincidence.

These unseen forces are powerful resources as you picture what you want your life to be like. When you set aside doubt, you set yourself up for an explosive jump toward your goal. The Higher Powers will rally to support you each time you choose trust over doubt.

I encourage you to use this chapter's strategy to welcome love and support into your life. The image is energized to help you focus on wonderful feelings. In the next chapter, we will discuss the power of gratitude. Even in the seemingly worst times, there are things to be glad for, and that thankfulness will raise your vibration.

Strategy

YOU ARE FULLY LOVED AND SUPPORTED

Settle into a favorite chair or sit on the floor, wherever is comfortable. As you look at this picture, imagine a brilliant, sparkling beam of white light between the image and the center of your forehead. Feel the peace of it and relax. Focus on the image for approximately a minute. Breathe in the words, "I am fully loved and supported."

Chapter Seven
Attitude of Gratitude

Chapter Seven

Attitude of Gratitude

Being grateful for your life may seem to be a difficult thing to do when you're caught up in how much you don't have. Instead of appreciating your job, your home, or your body, you may be constantly complaining about being passed over for a raise, all the repairs you have to do on your house, or all the weight you can't seem to lose. You're frustrated with the other drivers caught in the daily traffic jam, and you may be angry at God because this is not the life you wanted.

> *How to live life:*
> *pause, find something to appreciate, repeat.*

But as we learned with the law of attraction, this kind of attitude only serves to bring you more misery. The Universe is listening, and if what it hears are your worries about losing your job or getting fatter, those things are more likely to happen. When you are discontented, that is the vibration you are sending out.

Being grateful for what you have seems almost simplistic, but it affects many aspects of your life. If you resent your boss or hate what you have or don't have, you cannot attract something better into your life. You're working against what it is you want. It's like putting up a stop sign and saying, "I just want more things to resent. That's all I want to attract." If your focus is on resentment or what you *don't* have, you will end up with even more lack.

Jealousy Never Helps

It works the same with envy. If you are jealous or envious of the good that another person has, you can end up worse off than you are now. This happens because your personal vibration has dropped to the low point of envy. You now begin to attract to you things that match that low vibration, which is exactly opposite to the good that you want to have in your life. It is essential to be in an appreciative state or at least a neutral state to be in the positive flow of receiving.

If you can find genuine happiness for your friend who got promoted, and if you have gratitude for what you already have, then what you have will grow into something much more splendid. If you are grateful for what you do have—a job that pays benefits, a safe home to live in, a healthy body—you open yourself up for more abundance, like an unexpected raise that allows you to renovate your home or join the gym.

Stop Complaining

Pay attention to your thoughts throughout the day. Did you know that most thoughts are useless? We tend to want to have our minds stay busy, which really isn't helpful in moving you in the right direction. A busy mind shuts down creativity and guidance. It's like having a house filled with clutter. It makes everything more difficult.

Begin to notice how much energy you spend on complaining and judging. When you notice a complaint pop into your mind, stop the thought! Accept whatever is happening in the moment, or at least stop the negative thought. Not only will this change your current situation quickly, it will increase your personal vibration to a level where change comes easily.

Try to observe the world around you and yourself without judgment. Instead of complaining about the car you drive, imagine getting into the car you desire. Just pretend. When I did this, I ended up with the car of my dreams.

Instead of seeing a man with dirty clothes, you can simply see a man walking into the hardware store for more gardening tools. Remove judgment! It only holds you back from the life you want.

An attitude of gratitude offers many benefits. People who give thanks on a daily basis say they feel more alive and are kinder to others. They even sleep better and have stronger immune systems. You would be surprised at how feeling gratitude for things you often take for granted can improve the way you view the world. You can be grateful for things like indoor plumbing, having legs to walk with, hearing the birds chirping outside your window, or watching a beautiful sunset.

There are many things to be grateful for, no matter where you are in life and even at your bleakest times. I've experienced many positive changes throughout my life because of my attitude of gratitude.

Tears of Gratitude

My husband works on the family ranch where we live. We were very fortunate that living on the ranch rent-free was a benefit of his position. However, we knew that one day the ranch would sell, which would mean we would lose our home.

We didn't have close to the income to even consider buying the ranch or anything else. I desperately tried to think of ways we could buy the portion of the ranch where our home sits. I brainstormed with a friend, and we came up with ideas like a pumpkin patch, a corn maze, and a Christmas tree farm, or maybe offering space for events. I thought of creating a living museum. The ideas flowed, but although they were fun, none of them would have supported a mortgage. The dream of owning this property seemed hopeless.

Spontaneously, I melted into a state of gratitude for all that was around me. The feeling inside was that it was already mine.

One day, I was walking in the orchard behind my house, as I often do, and I paused to simply take in the beauty of the scenery. The temperature that day was perfect. I felt the warm breeze gently touching my skin. The sun was low, and everything glowed. It took my breath away. Spontaneously, I melted into a state of gratitude for all that was around me. The feeling inside was that it was already mine. With tears flowing and in total gratitude, I took in the beauty and wonder of life. I stood there until the moment passed, and then I walked home as usual.

Within days, I received a miracle: an unexpected check in the mail. The check provided us with the funds to purchase the ranch. Miracles do happen! Gratitude is an essential component to seeing miracles occur. By fueling experiences of gratitude in your life, you can begin to attract miracles.

I Love Fruit Trees

It's amazing how much my life has changed. As I followed many of the very same steps I have shared in this book, my life became a magnet for miracles. One day, I was driving down the road with my husband, and we passed one of those booms that raise a worker up high to work on the electrical wires. And I said, "Honey, you need one of those." The very next day, a friend stopped by and gave him one. We still use it today.

A few years ago, I wanted to plant fruit trees in the yard. My husband was against the idea because they get so messy. Shortly after that conversation, I discovered that a lilac bush I had planted years earlier had apricots on it. It has become a full-sized apricot tree now. Then on the other side of the ranch where we live, two plum trees appeared.

I'd like to share with you a strategy about being grateful that has worked for me many times in my life. Gratitude exercises are easy to use and take up a minimal amount of time. In the next chapter, I invite you to find the courage to live your dreams. You'd be surprised how taking action and truly believing in the manifestation of your desires can change your life.

Strategy

BE GRATEFUL!

Living in a state of gratitude is an absolutely optimal way to live life, and it is quite the opposite of the way many people live. Most people live in perpetual worry and fear. Why not do the opposite? If you choose to take on your mind, you will be continually surrounded by things for which you are grateful—and in turn, your state of gratitude will attract more things, ideas, beliefs, and experiences to be grateful for. I know sometimes it's a stretch to feel gratitude. However, you can train yourself to move from living in a state of fear and worry to a state of gratitude very quickly.

Use a journal and set a timer for five minutes. Jot down things that you are grateful for without stopping for the entire five minutes. If you prefer, you can do this in your mind instead of writing. This is a great exercise to do before bed to set the stage for the next day. This might be more challenging if you have had a difficult day, but try it anyway.

Find even the smallest things to be grateful for. It might even be that the day is finally over. Be grateful that you have a place to sleep; be grateful that you have a new tool to help you access a path to happiness; be grateful that you can provide food for your dog. There is so much to be grateful for in life, and it's so easy to take it all for granted. Every day as you do this exercise, you will steadily increase your personal vibration and surprisingly find more and more things to be grateful for. You will automatically look for things in life to be grateful for. What a great way to live!

Chapter Eight
The Courage to Live Your Dreams

Chapter Eight

The Courage to Live Your Dreams

The courage to live our dreams is within all of us, though we may not realize it. We were taught early on to follow rules, behave a certain way, and believe in certain things. We were given a framework—a structure to live within. All of this robbed us of the magic in ourselves. Between the way we were raised and the expectations of society, we've lost our courage. We've lost who we really are.

We came into this world to live a miraculous life. It should be the norm. But we've been turned into robots, for lack of a better word, by even the most loving of parents. Their role was to raise responsible adults. How can children grow into responsible (predictable) adults if they believe in something that cannot be seen or perceived? Our parents viewed it as childish make-believe ... which it actually was. Make-believe turns into make-happen. Our parents just didn't understand that. Our entire society has lost its magic. What an enormous loss!

So how can you find the courage that is hidden deep inside? By trusting your Higher Power. Your mind may have a hard time wrapping itself around the concept of surrendering to the Universe. It just sounds too good to be true. You may think that surrendering is a passive act and that acceptance to get what you want means simply sitting around and making wishes. But it's not as easy as a wish. While it is important to visualize what you want out of life, just seeing it in your mind's eye doesn't guarantee success. You have to get in touch with your heartfelt desires. You have to take action. And you have to be open to the powers of the Universe.

Trust in the Power of Pursuit

Most people confuse wishing and wanting with pursuing. While making wishes simply expresses your desires, pursuing shows the Universe that you are ready to achieve your goals. Dreams begin to crystallize into reality when they are pursued. The world behaves differently when you take action and go after what you want. The dream moves in your direction as you move toward it.

Remarkably, action taken, even in the *opposite* direction, is better than no action at all. It's easier to steer a train that is already in motion than one that is stopped. Action starts the energy moving. It alerts the Universe that you are ready for your next step. It's an absolute essential step to transform a dream or an idea into reality.

Get Uncomfortable

You won't necessarily feel all warm and fuzzy when the time for your explosive jump is near. Uneasiness is a predictable reaction when a quantum leap is underway. You will be thrown out of your comfort zone, and you must be ready and willing to take on the unexpected.

Prepare yourself to cover some unfamiliar terrain and encounter obstacles you've never faced before. This is probably the only part of the process that you'll have any kind of control over. You are the one riding the situation. You don't really have full control over it, but you can prepare by knowing what your goals are and where you're going. Learn from your mistakes and keep pursuing your dreams.

> *Prepare yourself to cover some unfamiliar terrain and encounter obstacles you've never faced before.*

Getting Honest

It takes courage to be honest with yourself. You may think you are being completely true to yourself, but are you saying yes to people when you really want to say no? Are you continuing to invest time in toxic relationships? Is that really the job you want to be doing?

To truly be happy, you must become your true, authentic self. When you're not, you're using a tremendous amount of energy to maintain a false persona. This is especially true if you were trained, as most kids are in childhood, to do as you're told, finish what's on your plate, always help others, and be a good little girl or boy. None of these things allow you to be who you are. We were trained to please others and deny who we are at an early age.

I'm not saying you should quit your job or refuse to ever help anyone. This is more about looking inside yourself at who you are. It certainly takes courage to be this honest.

It's crucial to keep going even when you are afraid, especially when you are taking big steps in personal growth. Fear is normal. It may be uncomfortable or alarming, but you can welcome it because it's a reminder that you are indeed growing. You can set it aside or you can rationalize it, but do whatever is necessary to move beyond it.

Being aware of your fear will help you come from a more authentic place. Your relationships will improve, more opportunities will arise, and you'll be happier.

Becoming Present

It also takes courage to live in the present. It's often easier or more comfortable to worry about the future or regret the past because that is what you have always done. But focusing on what's in front of you and around you in the moment will help you stay focused and ready for the quantum leap.

You can practice this by using a mindfulness meditation—the practice of purposefully paying attention to the present, neutrally and nonjudgmentally. Focus your attention on the present: for instance, on your breathing or by staring at an object like your hand or a candle. As thoughts come through your head, acknowledge and accept each thought, feeling, or sensation that arises. Do so without judgment. Then bring your focus back to your breathing or the object. This keeps *you* in control of your emotions by turning off your thinking left brain, the part of your mind that is creating the mind chatter, and turning on the feeling right brain, the part where you experience well-being and peace.

Sometimes you may need to change your thinking or change your focus when it comes to thoughts that drive you toward eating that chocolate cake, for instance. You need to take charge of your mind and allow the unwanted thoughts to pass by. Just let them go. In this way, you are now present in a new moment, one where you oversee your mind. Ultimately, you achieve a deeper self-acceptance, self-esteem, and self-love that will translate into greater inner peace and greater compassion for others. The outcome of this is living a life of purpose—a life of miracles.

I invite you to use the next strategy to find courage. Affirmations are easy to use in any situation and help you focus on positive thoughts as well as create uplifted feelings. In the next chapter, we will discuss how we can deal with setbacks along the path to our desires. It's not always pleasant, but these difficulties are often a gift in disguise.

Strategy

AFFIRMATIONS TO FIND YOUR COURAGE

Using affirmations is a wonderful way to boost your confidence and fight the self-defeating thoughts that threaten to sabotage the work you have been putting in toward your goals. You can repeat your affirmations while you are meditating, walking, or journaling. You can write them on Post-it notes to put throughout your home. There are many courage affirmations out there, and you'll probably come up with some on your own, but here are a few examples:

- I have what it takes.
- I love my life!
- I am a magnet for miracles.
- I easily take my next steps.
- The Universe has my back.
- My wisdom increases every day.
- My positive attitude attracts good things.

Chapter Nine
Shaking Things Up

Chapter Nine

Shaking Things Up

If you're like the rest of us, you hate to make mistakes, and you are disappointed when things don't go your way. If you fail, you worry what others will think of you. You think you're no good because you've been fired, rejected, or told you were wrong. After all that challenging work of bumping into the windowpane only to find there isn't an opening, that can be excruciating! No wonder you get stuck in a rut and find it hard to go on to the next level.

The fact of the matter is, setbacks are a part of life. As the saying goes, "You're only human." That doesn't necessarily mean that failing is a bad thing. It's a part of success. You learn what works and what doesn't—what you want and what you don't want. The contrasts of life are what help move you to your next level. Look at setbacks as a gift rather than something bad. Remind yourself that there is always something better on the way.

These temporary difficulties help you grow so you are prepared for bigger roles, greater responsibility, and greater wisdom to handle your impending success. It's the part of the yin and yang of realizing your dreams. Failure is not evidence that you are on the wrong path or that you should give up on your quest. Failure can be a sign of progress. You can't have quantum leaps without problems or challenges. You don't need to dwell on the possibilities, but you may encounter some setbacks along your journey.

Failure can be a sign of progress.

It Might Get a Little Messy

According to Kantar's Law, it always seems like you've failed while you're going about trying to succeed. Whenever you take on a new adventure—such as transitioning to a new job, taking on a particular project, or learning how to do something you've never done before—there will always be an adjustment period. You're going to make mistakes as you are being trained for your new job. The plans for the project may have to be altered as you deal with Murphy's Law. And maybe learning how to speak Italian is difficult; it may not seem as romantic as it did when you decided to take the course. These are the times when we doubt ourselves and wonder if the decision that brought us to this place was the right one.

But you can't bake a cake without getting the kitchen messy. When you clean a closet that hasn't been touched in years, the first thing you do is pull everything out of it, creating a big pile of junk in the middle of the room. Pritchett points out that, on its way to the moon, a rocket will go off course several times before it gets it right. So essentially, it encounters many setbacks before it reaches the moon.

I have failed more than anyone I know. Life is not necessarily a smooth and predictable ride. Rarely is the path to success a straight line. But obstacles and setbacks are great indicators that success is near.

Rarely is the path to success a straight line. But obstacles and setbacks are great indicators that success is near.

Obstacles Shake Things Up

When something does not go as planned, it might be a good thing. Without setbacks, you would simply be moving along in incremental steps and nothing would change. But when you encounter setbacks, they shake things up and give you a new perspective. That helps to make way for those quantum leaps that will propel you to victory.

It probably feels like things are out of your hands when you fail at something, because what you worked so hard at didn't give you the desired results. Or you may feel like the many roadblocks you encountered are signs that your goal is just not attainable. But you do have control over this aspect.

Without setbacks, you would simply be moving along in incremental steps and nothing would change.

When you fall short of a goal, you can give in to feelings of disillusionment and become unmotivated—or you can step back from the situation and see it in a new light. The solution may have been building up in your brain all this time, but sometimes you need the contrast to show you a different path. You're so wrapped up in what you're doing, you don't realize you need to change gears or consider things from a different angle. For many people, this is when they are at their most creative.

When problems show up, remember to trust that the Universe has your back. The problems that occur on the way to your dream coming true are there to help you grow and develop skills you'll need as your success manifests. A temporary difficulty is a sign of progress.

What Is Success?

When I first started writing this chapter, I wanted to make sure I did not focus too much on anything that might be described as failure. After all, it's so important to focus on the positive aspects of your life and the dreams you hold in order to move ahead. So let's balance out all this talk of setbacks and shaking things up by considering success. What is success? How do *you* define success?

Success could be making a lot of money or running your own business. There are incremental successes throughout your life—like paying the bills, redecorating your house, raising funds for the PTA, or finishing a college term paper. And there are big things like publishing your own book, inventing a new product, or finishing a marathon in record time. There are many mainstream successes that others may expect from you, but figure out how *you* define success. It doesn't matter what anybody else thinks as long as it's something close to your heart.

Let Go of the "How"

One of the easiest mistakes to make when going after a dream is to think about how it is going to happen. If you know everything you need to know to make your dream come true, your dream isn't big enough. When you focus on how to make your dream come true, you are sending a message to the Universe letting it know that you don't need its help. You are shutting down the very power that can make your dream happen.

Don't limit yourself to what you think you can achieve and let go of what others think you can accomplish; choose something better than you think is possible. Don't settle for something you think you can attain; choose something you passionately want. It won't make any sense to your mind that it's possible to have this, but that's all right. You can prepare your thinking. It's time to retrain your mind so it will relax and allow the universal mind/substance to make things happen *for* you and *through* you. This is one of the most life-changing concepts you can possibly learn.

This kind of revamping of the brain is the exact opposite of how we were taught as children. This concept doesn't create a dreamer. Instead, it will awaken the Power of the Creator in you. It will help you find who you really are. This is what life intended for you. You are powerful beyond measure and can create a life you love.

Choosing a Better Thought

You pay attention to what you eat. You make sure you brush your teeth. You care about how you look. You exercise to keep your waistline trim and tone your muscles. But do you pay enough attention to what you think?

If you've ever stopped to really listen to your thoughts, you may find some disparaging words about yourself or about others. These thoughts may seem to have evidence backing them up or be caught up in a time-loop of comments you've heard through the years. But your thoughts are not personal. They are just there. And believe it or not, you have control over your thinking. You don't have to believe your thoughts when they say something is impossible or you aren't worthy of success.

Being in charge of your thoughts is essential. If you are not in charge, you become a victim of default thinking. The circumstances of life will be in charge, and they will dictate how things will be. That's a scary way to live!

When you pay attention to your thinking and you think in a certain way, you are in charge of the circumstances of your life. By learning to listen to your thoughts and let the negative ones fall away, you'll discover a great deal. You'll find you are luckier. Opportunities are placed at your feet. New clients come out of nowhere. Unexpected income shows up.

You'll realize that you have the support of the Universe, and you'll feel that. You won't feel like you arwe in this alone. You won't be scrambling to make your rent. And one of my favorites: you won't be kept awake by worry. All you have to do is choose a better thought.

I offer the next strategy to help you deal with setbacks by replacing those nonproductive thoughts. In the next chapter, we'll talk about genuine acceptance and learning to trust. When you know that Source is there for you, every action you take will have an even better outcome.

Strategy

REPLACING UNWANTED THOUGHTS WITH POSITIVE DECLARATIONS

A very powerful way to stop unwanted thoughts is to replace the unpleasant thought with a positive one. You can do this by saying the new thought aloud, writing it down, or repeating it silently in your head. Doing all three will also give you fantastic results. As you repeat these affirmations, over time the replacements will become second nature, and you'll no longer have to battle the negative thoughts. Here are some examples:

- Change "Money never comes to me" to "I'm a money magnet."
- Change "I constantly make mistakes" to "Every day and every way, I'm getting better and better."
- Change "Dealing with money is misery" to "Money loves me."
- Change "I am unworthy" to "I am enough."
- Change "Others don't like me" to "I love myself and I love others."
- Change "No one values my opinion" to "I am worthy of respect."
- Change "I have failed" to "This is a temporary setback."

Chapter Ten

Genuine Acceptance

Chapter Ten

Genuine Acceptance

What does it take to be in a place of genuine acceptance and trust the process? For me, the foundation was built using energy work and finding my own steps to support my journey, like some of the things I have shared in this book. To transform your life, it's important to find ways to completely and sincerely trust Source, God, or the Universe. Everything happens for a reason, and you can trust that the process of life is here to serve you.

It goes beyond just saying that acceptance comes from faith in a Higher Power; you really must believe it in your heart. It's almost indescribable, the feeling you get the moment you truly realize what the world wants to give you. It instantly lifts you up and opens your eyes to possibilities as well as prepares you for that quantum leap.

This method is extremely effective and takes a lot less time than repeating over and over the same actions that don't work. Did you know that genuine acceptance is one of the fastest ways to have something change in your life?

Being Open to the Higher Power

As we touched upon in chapter 8, it may seem like accepting what the Universe has provided is passive or submissive. After all, we're told we must take action to make our dreams come true. But being comfortable with what is does not mean you should sit idly by; you still need to take action toward your goals. If there is something you can't control—for example, the weather, someone else's opinion, the decisions of upper management, or the state of the economy—you can accept it for what it is. Instead of spending your energy fighting things you cannot change, open yourself up to things you *can* change or take action on.

When you're getting a headache from bumping into that windowpane, step back and look around for another way. This lets the Universe know you are ready to move on. You are ready to learn from your failures and try something different. You can trust your Higher Power because it is always working on your behalf.

Allow Things to Move Through You

When feelings, thoughts, or situations arise that are painful or not constructive for achieving our goals, we often either completely ignore them or hold on to them tightly. Neither is conducive to getting you where you want to be. If you ignore a feeling, it fights to be heard, festering inside you until you can't hold it back. It explodes at the most inopportune times and may even affect your physical health. When you give a negative thought too much attention, on the other hand, it makes its home inside your head, constantly reminding you that it is there and affecting your decisions. The longer you hold on to a destructive thought like this, the harder it is to get rid of.

The Universe responds to everything you ask for, but it does not distinguish between what you consider good or bad. It doesn't hear, "I don't want to lose all my money." It just picks up on the vibration of "lose all my money." When you put your focus on something negative, you are telling the Universe you want more of the same in your life. You are actually creating the exact opposite of what you want.

> *When something happens in life that you do not like, ask yourself what opportunities this might bring. What's good about having this experience?*

The best way to deal with the thoughts that come through the monkey mind or chatter within your brain is to acknowledge the thought and then let it move through you. Allow it to voice its silly opinion and then nudge it along so it has no power over your life. The same thing is true of situations that you cannot control. Whether you fell on a slick restaurant floor, your financial investments took a plunge, or the dishwasher broke and flooded the entire kitchen, you can simply acknowledge that it happened and ask yourself, "Okay. Now what?"

When something happens in life that you do not like, ask yourself what opportunities this might bring. What's good about having this experience? You might not hear an answer right away, but you are opening yourself up to receiving the answer very soon. Stop trying to control things that are beyond your reach. It is such a misuse of your precious energy, creative talents, and focus.

Accept What Is

Learning to accept what is moves you through challenges very quickly. Otherwise, you end up staying where you are to learn a lesson from the challenge. Can you find something to be grateful for about this challenge? Maybe just the knowing that it will be over soon will help you find gratitude.

The challenge is there to move you to a better outcome. Get there faster by accepting and not resisting. Always focus on the thoughts that make you feel good and are productive in your quest for success.

Unconventional Approaches

Let's go back to that poor fly trying to get out the closed window. Sometimes for drastic change, you need to drastically change your method. We've all been programmed by that default setting that says there are certain ways of doing things. Many of us have grown up with concepts that worked for our parents but not necessarily for us. Back in the day, it was expected that you found a job with benefits and stayed there for twenty years or more until you retired. These days, people may have several jobs on their résumés—some because of problems with the economy, some because of family obligations, and some because they are pursuing their dreams. And more and more people are starting their own businesses with the help of the internet.

There is certainly nothing wrong with hard work. But the thing is, just because you have a goal you want to achieve and dreams to reach, that doesn't mean you must suffer. Think of this not so much as work but as putting your dreams in motion through inspired action. Quit trying harder. Unconventional success calls for unconventional approaches.

More of the same gives you more of the same. If you try harder at whatever you are now doing, you will end up with more of whatever *that* is. Which is fine, if you just want more of the same and you have the time and energy to put in to make that happen.

> **I'm inviting you to lean on your Divinity as your partner. Relax and put your trust in the Universe.**

However, you will reach a point where you can't try any harder. There won't be enough hours in the day, or you won't have enough energy, or you'll be stretched to the limit. Think of how the fly felt! It used all its life force to try to get through the glass. Working harder worked *against* it. Working differently would have worked *for* it. All it needed to do was fly a few feet away and exit through the open door.

I'm not suggesting that there isn't a need for your time and attention. But there isn't a need for frantic scrambling to figure things out. I'm inviting you to lean on your Divinity as your partner. Relax and put your trust in the Universe.

Let's do a process on trust. This will help balance and improve many areas of life that are influenced by too much trust or by a lack of trust. In the next and final chapter, I'd like to help you fall in love with your dream. Discovering your gifts within will help you refine your passion.

Strategy

FOCUS ON TRUST

Relax in a comfortable position. As you look at this picture, imagine a brilliant, sparkling beam of white light between the image and the center of your forehead. Focus on the image for approximately a minute. Breathe in the word *trust*.

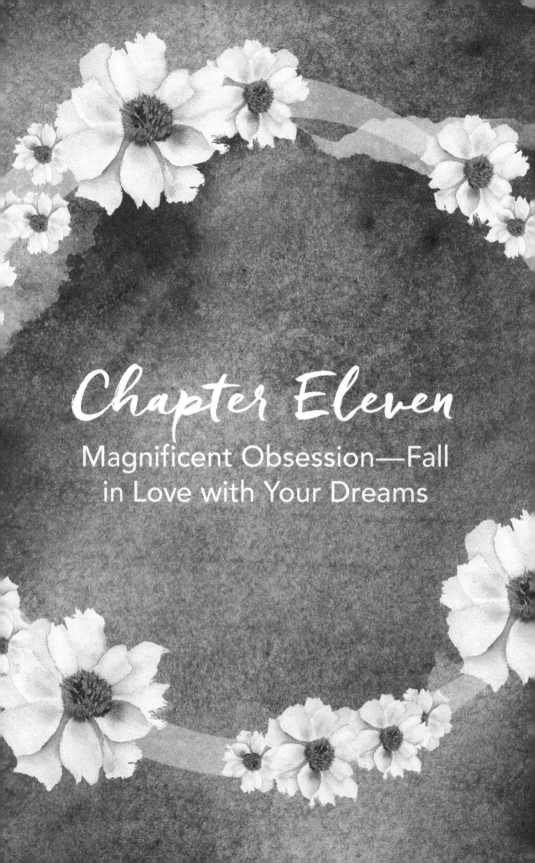

Chapter Eleven

Magnificent Obsession—Fall in Love with Your Dreams

Chapter Eleven

Magnificent Obsession—Fall in Love with Your Dreams

The Universe is at your service. It awaits you as you prepare for each explosive jump that will help you achieve your goals. But don't waste it on just any ol' desire or want that you may have. This is big! It has to be something you are wildly passionate about—a magnificent obsession. For a quantum leap to pick you up and thrust you forward, you must be in love with your dream.

Your Personal Gifts

You have many talents and abilities that you've never accessed. And you may not have even suspected that you have these skills because as you look around, you see others who have reached their goals. They've achieved their dreams. So obviously, they are the ones who are gifted. Right? Nope.

Those successful high achievers are different from you in only one way, according to Price Pritchett. They know about their gifts, and they use them. People you have deemed "winners" have unwrapped their gifts while many of yours are getting dusty sitting on a back-closet shelf somewhere, their pretty shiny ribbons fading.

Of course, you've unwrapped a few presents in the past few years. The talents, skills, and knowledge you've acquired already are gifts that you've claimed and used. But did you know that there are many, many more packages piling up in that closet waiting to be opened? You have an immense amount of untapped potential that can be a part of your quantum leap. You're going to be pleasantly surprised at the new talents you discover along your journey.

Passion

Finding these gifts involves knowing what you really want to do with your life. Passion is a very important part of this process. It energizes the heart and mind to make the quantum leap possible. This is why the dream you choose must be one that excites you—that you are passionate about.

Besides powering your dreams, passion will keep you on the path to success even when there are problems or doubts that may try to unbalance you. Fuel your passion with visions of a dream that are dramatic. The emotional intensity of your passion will ward off doubt, uncertainty, criticism, and failure. Let your deepest desires be your guide.

A key element to creating a huge leap is your excited anticipation of your desired dream. Believe, trust, and know that your dream is coming to you. Hold the feeling inside of excited anticipation whenever you think of your goal. It is essential to *feel* the feeling of what it would be like to already have your dream come true. With your magnificent obsession, you will be primed for that quantum leap.

Fuel your passion with visions of a dream that are dramatic. Let your deepest desires be your guide.

Make Your Move Before You're Ready

You don't plan your steps to get ready for a quantum leap. You make the leap, and you fine-tune as you go. Just begin. This is the same advice I give to people just starting out in business. First you act, and then you work out the details.

"Getting ready" is a stalling tactic. It's the reason so many people fail in business. And that's what society teaches us—to plan and be prepared. New business owners want everything in place before they start. They use up all their energy and passion in the preparation, and then they are so overwhelmed by what they need to do first that they never begin. So make your move!

Look Inside for Opportunity

Everything you need is already inside of you. You have the vision. You have the knowledge. You have the ability to take action, even if you are not aware of it.

The next step is to listen and really pay attention to your inner knowing. This is your guide that will lead you to the next step, which will bring your dream closer.

Pay attention to the little nudges you receive. Perhaps you will have an idea one day that shopping at the market across town sounds more appealing for whatever reason. Or you have an urge to approach someone to start a conversation and you usually prefer not to socialize. Or a relative pops in your mind, and you decide to call and just check in.

> *You have the vision. You have the knowledge.*
> *You have the ability to take action.*

This inner knowing doesn't always make sense. It isn't likely that you will see any connection between your guidance and your dream until you look back. But what you might begin to notice are opportunities presenting themselves. You might also notice synchronicities happening. Those are always fun! For me, synchronicities like checking the time and often seeing 11:11 are a reminder that I'm on the right track.

Feel welcome to try out this chapter's strategy on creating your vision.

Strategy

YOUR DREAM VISION

Imagine what you would like your life to be like. What kind of house are you living in? What kind of job are you working at? What kinds of things are you enjoying? Who are you socializing with? Write down ten items that describe your vision. As you read each one, think about how it feels as if it were happening right now. You may also come up with things that you didn't even know you were interested in. With an open mind, you will attract what the Universe has to offer and what your true passions encompass.

Conclusion

Feel Your Dream

Conclusion
Feel Your Dream

Life may throw all sorts of challenges and roadblocks your way. Economies may fail. People may disagree with you. Mother Nature may make you regret not bringing your umbrella. Just when you think you've got it all figured out, the Universe may step in and say, "Nope. That's not going to work." And it seems unfair. *Why is this happening to me? Nothing is ever going to work. This is too hard!*

But it really is so much easier than you realize. Remember, *you* are on purpose. There is a reason for you. You weren't just tossed in the ocean so your Higher Power could sit back and laugh, waiting for you to sink or swim. You were given this gift of life as well as all the resources to live the life you want to live. It may not always go as you planned, because the Higher Power knows what it's doing. Sometimes the Universe has to nudge you in a different direction, but it will take you to your most passionate dreams or something better if you are willing to surrender and trust the process.

> ***Our life always expresses the result of our dominant thoughts.*—Soren Kierkegaard**

It has so much to do with your thinking and what your story is. On a daily basis, how you see the world—whether in a positive or negative manner—will affect the possibilities of achieving your goals. And then once you see yourself and everything around you in an optimistic way, you will achieve more than you ever thought possible. Learn to expect the unexpected.

This information is powerful. It can create absolute miracles in your life. The key is to keep it in the forefront of your mind. Continue to read your goal as often as possible. Really *feel* the feeling of what it will be like when your dream comes true.

Continue to take action in the direction of your dream. You might want to create a vision board or a community of like-minded people where you can inspire one another. Allow the passion of your desire to keep doubts at bay. Fear and doubt are inevitable. When you start to experience fear, catch yourself as soon as you notice it and surrender to a Higher Power. The Universe really does have your back.

Abundance Everywhere

While you are waiting with pleasant expectation for the abundance of money, career advancement, or romantic love, remember to look at all the abundance you already have. Notice all the hues of the trees and shrubs as you walk in the park or drive down your street. You are surrounded by an abundance of color wherever you look. Appreciating abundance in any form attracts greater abundance to you. Notice the abundance of fruits and vegetables at the market. The displays are overflowing with beautiful and abundant produce.

Here's a secret for increasing your vibration and abundance: when you notice something of beauty, pause and inhale to breathe in the beauty of it. Really spend a moment taking it all in. It is as if you are quenching the thirst of your soul when you notice beauty and breathe it in.

There is so much out there that we take for granted, like the abundance of oxygen, the abundance of clouds, the abundance of music, and the abundance of love. There is so much beauty out there, and it's easy to find.

Delicious Anticipation

Living in gratitude and saying yes to life are what complete our foundation so we can live in anticipation of miracles. Excited anticipation is what attracts miracles. Anticipation is so powerful! It is the grown-up version of the eager expectation that a child has on Christmas Eve.

Excited anticipation is what attracts miracles.

Your anticipation that good things are always coming your way will continue to open doors for you, move huge obstacles from your path, and provide far more than you ever thought possible. Life has waited so patiently to shower you with miracles. All that's needed is for you to be ready to receive them. You have what it takes, and now is the time.

Thank you for allowing me to accompany you on this journey. I wish you great success and much love.

About the Author

Debra Cummings is dedicated to sharing the miracles that have transformed her life. Her sincere wish is to inspire others to succeed. She believes that everything is possible and that we each have within us the spark to awaken to our fullest potential, our greatest joy, and our deepest connection.

Her interests include animals, farming, nature, technology, shoes, and a deep desire for a kinder, gentler way of life for people and animals. She lives in California with her husband, three dogs, two cats, and fifteen sheep.

You can find out more at simplepathtoamiraculouslife.com or on Facebook at facebook.com/debracummingsenergywork/.

Bibliography

Abraham-Hicks Publications. Accessed January 28, 2017. http://www.abraham-hicks.com/lawofattractionsource/index.php.

Bennett-Goleman, T. *Emotional Alchemy: How the Mind Can Heal the Heart*. New York: Harmony House–Random House, 2001.

"Carl Sagan Quotes." Goodreads. Accessed January 28, 2017. https://www.goodreads.com/quotes/601581-the-hindu-religion-is-the-only-one-of-the-world-s.

"Courage Affirmations." Affirm Your Life. Accessed January 28, 2017. http://affirmyourlife.blogspot.com/2009/07/courage-affirmations.html.

Cutler, Zach. "Failure Is the Seed of Growth and Success." *Entrepreneur*. November 6, 2014. https://www.entrepreneur.com/article/239360#.

"Dale Carnegie Quotes." Goodreads. Accessed January 28, 2017. https://www.goodreads.com/author/quotes/3317.Dale_Carnegie.

"Mark Twain Quotes." Goodreads. https://www.goodreads.com/quotes/548857-comparison-is-the-death-of-joy.

Marter, Joyce. "15 Affirmations: Find the Courage to Live the Life You Want." *The Huffington Post*. Last modified November 17, 2014. https://www.huffingtonpost.com/joyce-marter-/find-the-courage-to-live-the-life-you-want_b_5826674.html

"Meet Mary Morrissey." MaryMorrissey.com. Accessed 28 January 2017. http://www.marymorrissey.com/meet-mary-morrissey.

Oladipo, Wale. "15 Ways To Defeat Negative Thinking and Grow a Healthy Mind." MindBodyBreakthrough. Accessed January 28, 2017. http://waleoladipo.com/15-ways-to-defeat-negative-thinking-grow-a-healthy-mind/.

Pritchett, Price. *You Squared: A High-Velocity Formula for Multiplying Your Personal Effectiveness in Quantum Leaps.* Dallas, TX: Pritchett & Associates, Inc., 1996.

Tempesta, Daniela, LCSW. "Why You Should Stop Comparing Yourself to Others." *The Huffington Post.* Last modified February 16, 2014. https://www.huffingtonpost.com/daniela-tempesta-lcsw/comparing-yourself_b_4441288.html.

CPSIA information can be obtained
at www.ICGtesting.com
Printed in the USA
BVHW040211181022
649705BV00006B/78